I0606405

better together*

This book is best read together, grownup and kid.

a kids book about

a kids book about Goals

by Sean Oulashin

A Kids Book About
Editor Emma Wolf
Head of Design Rick DeLucco
Publisher Jelani Memory

DK
Senior Production Editor Jennifer Murray
Senior Production Controller Louise Minihane
Managing Editor Hazel Eriksson
Publishing Director Mark Searle

This American Edition, 2025
Published in the United States by DK Publishing,
a Division of Penguin Random House LLC
1745 Broadway, 20th Floor, New York, NY 10019

25 26 27 28 29 10 9 8 7 6 5 4 3 2 1
001—355678—Jan/2026

First published in Great Britain in 2025 by
Dorling Kindersley Limited, 20 Vauxhall Bridge Road, London SW1V 2SA
A Penguin Random House Company

The authorised representative in the EEA is
Dorling Kindersley Verlag GmbH. Arnulfstr. 124, 80636 Munich, Germany

A CIP catalogue record for this book is available from the British Library

ISBN 978-0-2417-8589-8

Printed and bound in China

www.dk.com

akidsco.com

This book was made with Forest Stewardship Council™ certified paper – one small step in DK's commitment to a sustainable future.
Learn more at www.dk.com/uk/information/sustainability

To my mom, for showing me
what it means to be disciplined.

To my dad, for always making
space for my curiosity.

And to Lexi, my wife,
for believing in me
every step of the way.

Intro
for grownups

Goals are everywhere. From school, to sports, to screen time—kids are often encouraged to "set goals" or "work hard." But too often, those conversations focus only on the finish line.

I wrote this book to shift that perspective.

As someone who's spent years teaching focus, motivation, and self-discipline, I've learned that the real magic of goal-setting is less about reaching the end—and more about everything you become along the way.

Yes, this is a book designed to help kids set big goals, but it's also about helping them understand how to grow, adapt, and learn through the process. It's about building confidence, learning from failure, and getting curious about who they're becoming.

My hope is that this book gives you and your kid a shared language to talk about goals together. Not as something to feel pressure around, but rather, something to imagine the possibility of.

My name is **Sean.**

I’ve been a **martial artist**, and a **magician**, and I’ve gotten **hundreds of millions of video views on the internet.**

Sound cool to you?

Yeah—I think so too!

But all of that didn’t happen overnight.

In fact, it was **way harder** than
I could’ve possibly imagined.

And there was **one thing**
that made it all possible.

It might seem really obvious, but
I think most people get it all wrong.

But before we dive into that…
let me tell you a story.

When I was 3 years old,
I became a martial artist.

Sounds young, but it's true!

My mom got me into it—**she was the head instructor, after all.**

I learned
the basics
of **blocking**,
punching,
and **kicking**,
and just
like that, **I was hooked.**

Right then and there, I knew:
I had to become a master,
just like my mom.

I showed up **every week for years**, training until it felt like my legs would fall off, until eventually…

I did it!
I became
a master.

→ I set a goal,

and I achieved it!

When I was a kid,
I thought that to achieve a goal,
you had to reach the finish line.

But I've realized that
what makes setting goals
amazing is that you

**learn things
along the way.**

Standing in front of my martial arts class to receive my new title wasn't what gave me the most joy (but it was pretty awesome!).

It was actually all the time I spent **studying**, **learning**, and ultimately **teaching** that led me to this feeling.

Pretty cool story, **right**?

Wanna hear another one?

Let’s do it.

I was 8 years old
when I was first introduced
to **magic**—and it

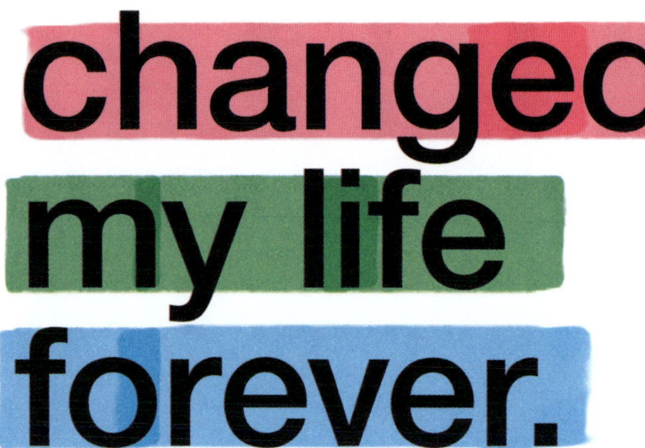

My dad got me my
very own magic book
for my birthday that year.

I read it cover to cover,
and before I closed the book,
I had already decided:

I was going to become a magician.

So, I **studied** hard,
practiced even harder,
and **performed** all the shows I could.

Then I did it—
I became
a magician.
It was amazing!

Do you want to know
what I remember the
most from that time?

**Learning how to make
videos with my dad.**

He taught me how to film videos of my card tricks, and then I shared them with other magicians around the world.

Oddly enough, that was a goal I didn't even have.

I learned that when
you're trying to achieve a goal,

something even more

amazing can appear,

if you’re open to it.

OK.

Martial artist,

magician,

what's next?

I was 24 when I discovered
how **powerful** the internet was.

I decided that I wanted to
change my life by setting
the **biggest**, **scariest**
goal I had ever set.

I wanted to post a video online,

for an entire year.

But not as a martial artist,
or a magician…just as me, **Sean**.

Before I knew it,
one of my videos went viral,

and just like that,
I had an audience.

I kept **posting**, and kept **growing**—
all the way until the end of the year.

365 days straight,

1 video per day.

ANO

GOAL

D

THER

OWN.

But, I gotta be **100% honest**—
that wasn't the coolest part.

I realized more than the attention,
what I really loved about
making videos was...

helping people in need with an important message.

So, I’ve done a lot of cool
stuff with my life so far.

And what made
all of these things possible
was the **goals I set**.

But here's what most people get wrong about goals.

The truth is…

goals can change

and GROW.

And more often than not, they should!

Really!

In fact, that's the whole point.

It's not just about what
you achieve when you reach
your goals, but all the things
you **gain along the way.**

Like…

the incredible journey **you go on,**

the life lessons **you learn,**

and the new goals that **grow with you.**

Ride a bike. Finish a painting. Touch your
how to breakdance. Ride a skateboard. Lea
language. Volunteer. Record a song. Save
Draw a picture every day. Sing a song. Exe
to animate. Learn how to code. Build a ca
Save for a new scooter. Give a complimen
Do ten push-ups. Read twenty minutes eac
your room every day. Tie your shoes. Start
records. Start a business. Learn how to mak
Learn how to swim. Learn a magic trick. Ea
to roller skate. Write a haiku. Donate unus

You might already have some goals. Co

Keep a journal. Keep a sketchbook. Organ
Learn origami. Practice multiplication. Play
how to catch a ball. Run a mile. Try a new f
a ceramic vase. Collect shells in a jar. Organ
Learn how to make a felt animal. Make a m
movie every day. Stretch every day. Learn
business. Call a family member. Write a lett
to yourself every day. Climb a tree. Pick u
Make a beaded necklace. Make a fort out
backyard. Go to the movie theater once a
to hula hoop. Try rock climbing. Learn how

. Do a cartwheel. Learn how to fish. Learn
ow to skip. Take care of a pet. Speak a new
ey. Learn an instrument. Write in a journal.
e. Help a friend. Start a garden. Learn how
oard spaceship. Earn one hundred dollars.
fifty jumping jacks. Beat a running record.
y. Start a collection. Make a collage. Clean
ook club. Listen to new music. Collect vinyl
ne. Learn how to make flower arrangements.
ore vegetables. Tie dye a t-shirt. Learn how
lothes. Finish a big puzzle. Learn a dance.
meal. **You might have hundreds of them!**
our room. Learn about your family lineage.
w board game. Learn how to juggle. Learn
Learn how to sew. Drink more water. Make
scavenger hunt. Learn how to rock tumble.
ture house. Sculpt a clay pig. Watch a new
v to throw a frisbee. Start a lawn mowing
a friend from far away. Say something nice
sh with a grownup. Learn how to crochet.
lows. Learn how to knit. Go camping in the
th. Learn how to use a camera. Learn how
ve. Make a toolbox. See your favorite band.

Maybe
you want to
become an
airplane pilot,

or run
a marathon,

or live in a big house with an incredible view.

Co

Those
are
great
goals
to
have.

Just remember to let your goals

change and

GROW, just like you do!

Outro
for grownups

After reading this book, your kid might be thinking bigger. Or they might be feeling a little overwhelmed. Both responses are OK.

The best thing you can do is meet them where they are. Ask what they're feeling excited about. Ask what feels hard. And most of all, remind them that it's OK to change their mind, start over, or take things slow.

Progress looks different for everyone. Some kids move fast. Others need more time to figure things out. What matters is that they feel safe to try, grow, and be seen in the process. You don't need to have all the answers. You just need to be curious alongside them.

Let this book be a starting point. A way in. Something you can return to when they're stuck—or when they surprise you with what they're ready to do next.

Because when a kid believes in their goals, they start to believe in themselves.

About The Author

Hey, I'm Sean Oulashin. I've spent my life chasing big ideas—whether that's becoming a martial arts master, learning magic, or making videos that reach millions of people online.

But no matter what I'm working on, one thing has always helped me grow: setting goals.

I care a lot about helping people (especially kids!) believe in themselves, focus on what matters, and build a life they're proud of. That's why I wrote this book.

I live in California with my wife, Lexi, and when I'm not making videos, I'm probably hiking, journaling, or traveling the world.

 @seanoulashin  @seanoulashin